MW00993831

A Pearl
of Great Price

Sharing the Gift of Meditation
by Starting a Group

Laurence Freeman

Medio
Media

Again the kingdom of heaven is like a
merchant looking for fine pearls; when he finds one
of great value he goes and sells everything
he owns and buys it.　　　(Matthew 13:45)

©2002 The World Community for Christian Meditation

ISBN 0-9725627-0-2

All rights reserved.
No part of this book may be reproduced, stored in a retrieval
system, or transmitted, in any form or by any means, electronic, mechanical,
photocopying, recording or otherwise without
the written permission of Medio Media.

Cover Image and Book Design by Types

Medio
Media

2002
Medio Media
15930 N. Oracle Rd., Suite 196
Catalina, Arizona 85739
520.825.4560
www.mediomedia.org

CONTENTS

Introduction

There is nothing simpler than meditation. There are no difficult theories to master or techniques to excel in. Only simple fidelity is needed – and fidelity to simplicity. But as anyone who has tried it knows, being simple isn't easy. We need all the support and inspiration we can get to persevere in what is a simple but demanding discipline.

This is where the group meditation comes in. It is a spiritual phenomenon and a source of great hope, especially in our unpeaceful and fear-ridden time, that small groups of people in more than 60 countries around the world meet weekly simply to meditate together. They gather in all sorts of places, from homes to churches to prisons, hospitals and places work, to share the practice that connects them, in silence, simplicity and stillness, to the ultimate source of life and peace. After meditating together they return to life charged with that energy of faith that comes from being in the presence of the One who promised to be with those who were open to him.

In one sense, of course, the meditation group is nothing new, but in another it is the most contemporary expression of and answer to the tremendous spiritual hunger that so characterizes our time. It is not surprising then that The World Community for Christian Meditation has become in these last 25 years a global spiritual family with a deep common experience and much wisdom to share about sharing the gift of meditation. You may have to step out on your own to start a group, but you will never be alone or without resources to help and encourage you.

But who exactly starts and leads meditation groups? Ordinary people, who need no extraordinary talent, only the faith to begin and the support of those who have gone before. So this little book offers encouragement and practical ideas about how one might not only begin a group, but sustain and nurture it along the way. And it suggests that such work is of utmost importance. Our world sorely needs the silent infrastructure of contemplation woven into its institutions and frenetic schedules. It needs the healing and transforming power that only the spirit can set free in us and among us.

I am grateful to many in our community who have helped in preparing this book – especially Carla Cooper, chair of our Guiding Board, Susan Spence, co-ordinator of the international Centre and Joe Doerfer, the Director of Medio Media.

Laurence Freeman, OSB

The Call of Jesus

'Jesus bent down and started writing on the ground with his finger'. This moment, in St John's Gospel, occurs after a crowd that had been about to stone a woman to death dispersed and the woman is left alone with Jesus. Like other great teachers of the Spirit in all traditions, Jesus lived what he taught and taught by the example of his own behavior. And time and again we see him teaching by silence. On another occasion he transmitted his teaching to a rich young man who found it difficult to renounce his possessions, by a direct and loving gaze. And again there were times when, in the face of contradiction and hostility, he kept a pure and truthful silence.

Compassionate presence, loving attention and truthful silence. These are still essential elements of the way we follow Jesus as our teacher and friend. He urged and empowered us to share in the work of teaching the good news. We are called to teach as our teacher teaches and to grow in relationship with him and likeness to him. The qualities of presence and silence are perennial truths of this journey. Of course, our individual personalities, like the culture that shapes us, makes each journey its own unique story. But the essential human quest, the challenges and the fruits of meditation, are the same for all at all times.

Everyone Is A Contemplative

To understand the meaning of the meditation and the meditation group we need to understand better what contemplation means. In ancient times the 'contemplative life' meant a life of privilege. Only those who were educated and sat on top of the social pile could afford the time and leisure for contemplation. Later in Christianity the contemplative life became more democratic and anyone in the church could follow it. But it meant giving up the ordinary vocations of marriage and work in the world for a celibate and cloistered life. Contemplation still seemed a gift that God gave only to an elite. It is curious how for centuries the universal teaching of Jesus was restricted to the few. Jesus called everyone to 'be perfect' in love and compassion like his Father, to leave self behind, to shed materialistic stress and anxiety, to find the 'rest' of contemplation in accepting his yoke. But the universal application of the essential teaching was forgotten or repressed or denied.

The first Christians however got the point. They listened to the gospel when it told them to pray without ceasing. They understood that contemplation is an essential, universal element of the human condition. Martha and Mary are sisters, two complementary dimensions of the person, not just two personality types. Without Mary's stillness at the center, sitting at the feet of the teacher and listening, we become like Martha,

7

irritable, complaining, discontented, distracted. In the end we are not even very productive in the work we do. In fact Mary and Martha are both working, one interiorly, the other exteriorly. Contemplation is not an escape from one's life's work. It is a part of our work and helps us to do the other part better. Mary and Martha are like two chambers of one heart. They don't just complement one another; they need each other to realize fullness of life.

Cassian on the Mantra

This is the verse that the mind should unceasingly cling to, until strengthened by saying it over and over again and repeating it continually, it renounces and lets go of all the riches of thought and imagination. Restricting itself to the poverty of this single verse it will come most easily to that first of the Gospel beatitudes: for he says: 'Blessed are the poor in spirit for theirs is the kingdom of heaven.'

– John Cassian (c 400 AD)
Conference 10:11

Why Meditation Groups Matter Today

Just as in an active project we usually need a team to support us with its diverse talents, so in the work of contemplation we need community. Meditation, as John Main knew, creates and reveals community. The meditation group is but an expression of this truth. There is nothing new about Christians coming together to pray. 'The whole group of believers was united, heart and soul; they joined in continuous prayer'. This was said of the small Jerusalem church that formed after the death and resurrection of Jesus.

And we can say the same about groups today. There has been in the last thirty years or so a revolutionary rediscovery of the tradition of Christian contemplation, not just for the cloistered few but also for ordinary men and women. This is not a merely academic discovery. The practice of meditation has awakened a new awareness that the contemplative dimension of prayer is open to each of us and invites everyone. Access is not restricted. It is a privilege of grace given by the Spirit to all. But like all gifts of the Spirit, we must do our part. If we are to live our particular vocation in daily life with depth and meaning, we must actively accept the gift, tending it with humble devotion and daily fidelity.

It is no news that Christianity is in a turbulent transition from a medieval to a modern mentality. If we listened only to the media and the sociologists we might conclude that the Christian church is in terminal decline. Certainly its structures and attitudes are going through a death process, but at the heart of the Christian view of death is the certain hope of resurrection. The Christian meditation group, therefore, is one of those positive and hopeful signs of renewed life, an authoritatively silent sign, that the spirit prevails.

Meditation is a universal practice that leads beyond words, images and thoughts into the faith-filled and presence-filled emptiness we call the silence of God. What is particularly Christian about it is the awareness that it takes us, in faith, into the prayer of Jesus himself. And when we share in the human consciousness of Jesus, who is simultaneously open to each of us and to God, we can begin to be truly open to one another. We can create and experience the growing union of persons we call community. As the fruits of the spirit appear – love, joy, peace, patience, kindness, goodness, fidelity, gentleness, and self-control – so also does the grace of recognizing Jesus in ourselves and in one another.

John Main

One of the most influential spiritual teachers of prayer of our time was the Irish Benedictine monk, John Main. He was born in England in 1926 and died in Canada fifty-six years later. For Fr. Bede Griffiths, writing soon after John Main's death, he was the 'most important spiritual guide in the church today'.

As a young Catholic diplomat in the Far East, John Main was introduced to meditation by a gentle Hindu monk, Swami Satyananda. Never swaying from his own Christian faith, John Main immediately recognized the value of this practice that deepened and enriched the other forms of Christian prayer. It was not until years later that he fully realized how deeply this silent prayer of the heart was rooted in his own Christian tradition. He saw with fresh eyes the teachings of Jesus on prayer. And he read anew John Cassian's vivid descriptions of the early Christian monks, the Desert Fathers and Mothers, who practiced and taught by their own humble example the simple discipline of the 'prayer of one word'. He saw how powerfully this discipline deals with the distractions that inevitably fill the mind, most obviously at the time of prayer but at other times as well.

In the mantra he saw the way to that stillness ('hesychia' as the eastern Christians call it) or 'pure prayer' that is 'worship in spirit and truth'. He saw how the discipline of the mantra purifies the heart of contradictory desires and unifies us. The place of unity is the heart where we find the deepest and most natural orientation towards God as our personal source and goal. He understood too how the mantra brings us to poverty of spirit, or the non-possessiveness, that Jesus set as the first beatitude, the primary condition of human happiness.

John Main soon learned through his own practice of meditation that the morning and evening discipline of meditation balances the whole day, every day of one's life, in an ever-deepening peace and joy. And more and more, he saw the connection between this experience of inner peace and joy with the Gospel and Christian faith. Prayer for him now appeared as much more than speaking to or thinking about God. It is being with God.

It is important not to try to invent or anticipate any of the experiences. I hope that, as you come back to the discipline every day, it will become clear that each of us is summoned to the heights of Christian prayer – each of us is summoned to fullness of life. What we need however is the humility to tread the way very faithfully over a period of years so that the prayer of Christ may indeed become the grounding experience of our life.

Moment of Christ

A Discipline Of Faith Made Easier

John Main also saw the quality of our relationships as the true measure of progress in meditation. He knew that progress was in the end an accomplishment of grace. But again, we must do our part. We must respond to the call of grace not with a mere technique, but with a discipline of faith. For John Main, as for the centuries-old Christian tradition he spoke from, a freely chosen discipline is the path to freedom not bondage. Spiritual discipline is a valuable necessity in the work of being free from the tyranny of egotism, compulsiveness, delusion and self-centeredness.

He was therefore always very clear that meditation is a way of faith and very practical about how and when it must be practiced. The minimal commitment to individual meditation twice a day and group meditation once a week is only the external aspect of the discipline John Main taught. He knew that most people begin the discipline of meditation half-heartedly or with a tremendous zeal that inevitably, like infatuation, dissipates. We begin, then stop and then begin again, often many times. It takes time, maybe years, for some people to incorporate the basic discipline of meditation in their daily lives.

That is just why a meditation group is so valuable. Not many people are so good at self-discipline entirely on their own. It takes time and continual encouragement to build a good habit. Through the support and example of others, we strengthen our insight that meditation is simple, but not easy; life-giving, not life-denying; and most of all, a way of love. For all these reasons John Main encouraged people who wanted to learn to meditate and to keep on meditating to cultivate the gifts of community that grow among those who share the journey of prayer. Hence the formation and persistence of more than a thousand groups of three or six or 20, meeting weekly in homes, offices, hospitals, hospices, prisons, colleges, schools, shopping malls, and even the United Nations Building.

John Main on the Mantra

The way we set out on this pilgrimage to 'othercentredness' is to recite a short phrase, a word that is commonly called today a mantra. The mantra is simply a means of turning our attention beyond ourselves – a way of unhooking from our thoughts and concerns.

Word into Silence

Sharing The Gift

$\mathbf{A}$t a certain point in your own practice of meditation it dawns on you that you have indeed received a pearl of great price. Your Martha has stopped complaining about Mary. You see that being comes before doing and gives all doing the character of love. Still you may feel uncertain and cautious about taking the next step. After all, you will say, 'I'm not a guru. I don't know much about it anyway. And on top of that I'm not very good at it. I can't teach anyone else'. These thoughts are a good sign that you probably are ready to share the gift. But how to begin?

The very first step is most likely becoming comfortable to bearing witness to the reality of your own practice. This hardly means taking on any kind of in-your-face evangelical fervor. Sometimes you meet someone who shares him or herself with you more deeply than usual and you think 'maybe they would be interested in meditation'. So mention it. Or someone asks you why you seem a little easier to get on with than before. Tell them. Or you're staying with friends and you need to get away for half an hour to meditate before the evening socializing. Explain where you're going. All this is a matter of discretion, of course. Fortunately meditation cultivates discretion and good judgment.

Starting a group is a step further. Again you may feel hesitation. 'I'm just a beginner,' you will say. John Main says we are all always beginners. 'But I'm not a teacher,' you will say. Yes but Jesus is. You have only to worry about being a disciple. Seeing yourself as student, a disciple of Christ who teaches you by meditating in you, with you and for you, is all the qualification you need to go ahead. Jesus encouraged his disciples to teach 'in my name', which means in his presence and with his spirit. You need to be humble, but never afraid. Furthermore you have a community and a tradition to support and help you.

First Steps: First Obstacles

So you begin where you are and as you are. If you belong to a parish or worshipping community, start there. Speak to the priest or pastor or parish council or fellow parishioners. Explain what this gift has come to mean to you. But be prepared for surprise, uneasiness, even suspicion. Remember that when many people hear about meditation for the first time they are likely to think you are describing something new and strange at best or, at worst, something quite alien or threatening. Stay calm and don't be put off! It does help, however, to be familiar with the most common misperceptions about meditation. Here are a few of the most common:

Meditation is not Christian. It is imported from Buddhism or Hinduism. Explain as best you can that meditation is a universal spiritual discipline, existing in most other religions, especially those older than Christianity. But the way of silent prayer is deeply rooted in the Christian tradition, historically, theologically, and scripturally. Your understanding of the tradition John Main handed on, especially as he describes it in *Word Into Silence* and *The Gethsemani Talks*, is invaluable here. Sharing these powerfully clear little books is an excellent way to build relationships of trust and help others grow in understanding and confidence that meditation is a way of prayer and faith. Two other effective resources that help others situate meditation firmly on Christian ground are the pocket-sized

Christian Meditation: Your Daily Practice and the video, *Coming Home*, which also tells the story of the World Community through the voices of individual meditators from around the world.

The mantra is not Christian. Another aspect of the fear that meditation is not Christian is discomfort with the mantra, both as a term and as the 'work' the tradition teaches us to do. Again there is strong and consistent teaching. There is John Cassian's pivotal disclosure of the key to desert wisdom in his magnificent 9th and 10th Conferences on Prayer: poverty of spirit, the humble recitation of a few sacred words, what he calls in Latin the 'formula, that helps us keep our attention on the Lord instead of ourselves'. The 14th Century classic, *The Cloud of Unknowing*, calls it the 'one little word' that helps us turn from distraction toward the silent mystery of God. John Main had the insight to call the sacred word a 'mantra' thus linking the specifically Christian tradition to the universal wisdom. 'Mantra' is, of course now an English word, too, according to the Oxford English Dictionary, despite its too-often use to describe the promises of politicians. Originally a Sanskrit word (the root tongue of most European languages) mantra refers to 'that which clears the mind,' a short scripture verse or sacred word used in a repetitive way to help deepen attention. The rosary, the words of the mass, blessings, and familiar, repeated prayers of all kinds are mantras in this sense. And finally, there is the authority of Jesus who tells us not 'to babble on,' but to go to your secret chamber and there pray not with your lips, but in silence to, as John

Cassian describes it, 'the searcher not of words, but of hearts'.

Meditation is dangerous. This most often comes from fundamentalists whose aversion to mystery and need for literal and absolute certainty often conceal a high degree of fear and repression of fear. They react angrily when they are affronted or frightened by anyone daring to question the certainty they hold as the very essence of true faith. They will say 'when you open yourselves up or blank your mind the devil will come in'. More likely, however, the devil will get a chance to come out! Negative feelings and shadowy thoughts may get released when repression is lifted. This is quite natural but it can be bumpy for a while. The literature of Christian contemplation offers many descriptions of this process and advice on dealing with it. Meditation practiced moderately and in faith is not dangerous. It is more dangerous not to meditate. Meditation is not about blanking your mind but about being poor in spirit, open to the indwelling presence. Christians who believe in the resurrection and the presence of Christ within them should above all approach meditation with confidence and hope.

Meditation is selfish. That's what Martha thought too. But Jesus said that Mary had chosen the 'better part'. His own example of life shows him balancing his periods of active ministry with times of withdrawal and quiet. Navel-gazing is selfish. Meditation is the purest work of selflessness we can do because it takes the attention off the ego's agenda. Gradually it becomes a habit, a way of life. And gradually we see that our prayer is not an alternative to action, but its very ground. We discover the inextricable relationship between being and doing, and the simple fact that our life is as good as our prayer. If the latter is only about us, so then will be the former. If meditation did not show its fruits in greater love and compassion – that would be the great objection, and a valid one. But as stressed before, the only true measure of the efficacy of meditation is 'am I growing in love?'

Meditation is just a relaxation technique. We hear more in the popular media about meditation as a way to lower blood pressure, raise body temperature, and increase beta waves. This should not be a surprise in a medical and scientific world that claims the primacy of chemical and biological determinants of human behavior and identity. There is of course documented evidence that meditation is an exceptionally effective way to relax and experience the physical and psychological benefits of reduced stress and anxiety. But these outcomes are merely lovely secondary benefits of what is first and foremost a way of prayer. We might say that modern science has finally caught up with ancient wisdom.

Whatever objections people may raise when you start speaking about starting a group, listen to them. Try to see where they are coming from. Don't be defensive or argumentative. And remember that most priests, for example, never had an introduction to contemplative prayer in their training. They were formed to think of themselves as administrators rather than spiritual teachers and so, humanly enough, they may indeed feel threatened or put off by a lay person talking about contemplation. And remember that you are *not* saying—and the tradition does not teach—that meditation is the only way to pray. Try to share your own experience of how meditation is not a substitute, but a support for, all other individual and collective prayer. It feeds Christian life in all its dimensions, bringing us back to the living truth of the Gospel with heightened appreciation or to it, with fresh wonder, for the very first time.

If you get a negative response to your suggestion about starting a group, respond to the rejection contemplatively. It will strengthen you. Consider whether you should wait and try again or reflect on other avenues, other places or communities you might explore. But you may well be lucky, too. You may find a strong openness, indeed gratitude, that you suggested it and eagerness to help you. Then what?

Getting The Word Out

Publicity means not hiding your light under a bushel. It doesn't mean you have to sell meditation as a product. John Main said it was caught rather than taught. Perhaps the very best way to begin is to organize and offer an introduction to Christian Meditation, featuring a brief talk and perhaps showing of the *Coming Home* video, to be followed by group meditation. You may do the introduction yourself, especially if you have had the opportunity to attend a School for Teachers session in your area, or you may also be able to invite a leader from an existing group nearby or another volunteer in your area who would be happy to team up with you. Many regions have individuals so designated to help with new group formation. The introduction may be repeated at various intervals along the way, and can be organized to suit any circumstance: church, home, school, or business.

Making use of examples available through the School for Teachers, as well as descriptions in the Community's many other fliers and brochures, prepare a simple one-page description of the essential facts: *what, why, when (and how long), where, and who.* Describe the key points honestly and briefly. Remember that the combination of the words, 'Christian' and 'meditation' and 'group', speak pretty strongly for themselves. This 'one-pager' can serve as a communications resource in itself, a simple flier to distribute or even mail to selected others. It will also help you keep your facts together for other kinds of communications:

phone calls, e-mails, faxes, brief notice in the appropriate in–
house publications, like the parish bulletin and/or newsletter.
You can also consider a poster in a key location or a notice in the
local community newspaper. And remember, wherever you set
your introductory session, be sure to let your friends who are
interested know. Encourage them to join you and to pass the
word along. Finally, if your diocese has a spirituality commission,
make contact with its leadership. Whether or not your
introduction or group will be held in a church setting, members
of the spirituality group may very well give you critical moral
support, as well as offer helpful suggestions.

Where?

It is important to find a place where you can meet regularly each week. It should be as quiet as possible and be a suitable size. Moving from place to place each week can be disruptive. Having a choir practicing or a TV playing next door can be excellent tests of discipline now and then, but if it's every week, it's far less fun. Use your negotiating skills to ensure stability of place. It would be ideal if you can get a room or space allocated permanently for contemplative use alone, but that is rarely possible and not necessary. What you can do is create a space each week that is special. All that is required to transform an ordinary place into a sacred one is, in most cases, a single candle, a little music, and the group leader arriving just a few minutes early to prepare the room.

I meditated once in a crypt of a church in the business district of a big city. A steady core group of people working nearby met once a week during their lunch break. The leader of the group arrived before the others to put out the chairs in a circle around a simple candle. He also brought a small portable tape player. People arrived quietly as music played softly. They started punctually, listened to a brief taped teaching, meditated, shared a few words and went back to work. The candle was blown out, chairs were put away and in a moment there was no sign – except the energy of peace – that there had just been a group of meditators sitting together in stillness and silence.

Groups now meet in homes, apartments, schools, churches, rectories, religious communities, community centers, Christian Meditation Centres, chapels, universities, prisons, government office buildings, a department store, senior citizens' homes and factories.

Reciting the mantra brings us to stillness and to peace. We recite it for as long as we need to before we are caught up in the one prayer of Jesus. The general rule is that we must first learn to say it for the entire period of our meditation each morning and each evening and then to allow it to do its work of calming over a period of years.

The day will come when the mantra ceases to sound and we are lost in the eternal silence of God. The rule when this happens is not to try to possess this silence, to use it for one's own satisfaction. The clear rule is that as soon as we consciously realize that we are in this state of profound silence and begin to reflect about it we must gently and quietly return to our mantra.

Gradually the silences become longer and we are simply absorbed in the mystery of God. The important thing is to have the courage and generosity to return to the mantra as soon as we become self-conscious of the silence.

Introduction to **Moment of Christ**

When?

Most groups meet in the late afternoon or evening when people are on their way home from work or after they have eaten and then come out again. For working people this is often the best time apart from lunchtime groups near their workplace. But for retired people, homemakers, mothers with young children or the sick, a morning or afternoon time can be best. Different times of the day or week will attract different types of people. In some communities, there are meditation groups meeting several times a week or every day at different times to respond to people's different situations.

Choose a time best suited to your schedule, as your regular presence is essential. It is very important for you as the group leader to be as faithful as you possibly can, especially in the first months as well as during the summer when numbers often drop off. If you cannot be there, arrange for someone else to take your place. This not only ensures continuity, but can help others in the group realize their own potential for leadership. Be sure to stay with the announced times for beginning and ending; the time together builds confidence and stability. A group can easily be completed in an hour or less.

How Many?

Don't measure the group's success by the number of participants. The size of the group is really not important. Two or three faithful meditators make a good meditation group. As C. S. Lewis once said to a clergy conference he was addressing, 'the Lord said feed my sheep don't count them'. Nonetheless the tendency to judge success by numbers is deeply engrained in us. Just catch yourself when you start doing it. Normally a group experiences a reduction in numbers after an initial influx of enthusiasm. Expect this and focus on those remaining. This is the vital point where a community of faith begins to form. Some of those who drifted away may have been greatly enriched by their brief encounter with the group. Some may be meditating on their own. Others may come back when, in a year or two, they see that the group is still meeting and its example of steady fidelity inspires them to start again.

The discovery we make in meditation is that the repetition is not mechanical but creative. Just as the practice itself, starting and leading a group is a creative work. So don't judge it materialistically. The kind of growth that concerns us in meditation groups is spiritual not numerical. With growth in depth there follows in time an expansion in numbers, if not in your particular group, then in the creation of other groups meeting at different times and places. A small meditation group in each parish, for example, would be a quantitative goal worth pursuing. From time to time, of course, you can cast the net on the waters again and publicize a new introductory series of groups or revamp the standing notice you have on a poster or in a bulletin. But, remember, even if the group stays small it will find strength from belonging to the wider national and global community.

What Do We Do When We Get There?

Keep it simple. Keep words to a minimum. Let it be what it is – a meditation group, not a discussion group or a therapy group or a prayer group of another sort. The most important part of the group is the period of meditation. Always keep the silence central and the rest will fall into place. Here are a few practical hints for how to ensure a contemplative environment and the most meaningful experience for all.

The Preparation. As people arrive let them feel welcomed but also make it gently clear that they are entering a sacred place and time. Ten minutes before the start time put on some quiet music, light a candle, and gently ask people to be stop talking. People generally need to be encouraged in this, because many feel they might be unsociable by not chatting with others. At the start time turn off the music and welcome people, especially newcomers.

The Teaching. An ideal way to give the teaching is to play one of the many taped talks of John Main. These extraordinary teachings were originally given to meditation groups very like the one you are now sitting in. The talk is not a sermon or a lecture but a spiritual preparation for a time of contemplation. Listening to the talk involves not just the mind but also the heart. It works by placing you in the optimum frame of mind and attention for the time and work of meditation. In this way the tapes never become repetitious, however many times you may listen to them. But as there are about 200 of them, you have plenty of time to do the rounds.

There are some talks that are specifically introductory (such as side A of the five twenty-talk *Communitas* series) and some are for more experienced meditators (such as side B of that series). *The Essential Teaching*, another set of John Main tapes, is comprised of three introductory tapes, published in book form as *Word into Silence*. The third of these tapes *Twelve Talks for Meditators* has proved very popular for groups. *In the Beginning* is a series of introductory talks while *Being on the Way* is for more experienced meditators. *Door into Silence* and *Word Made Flesh* are also sets of both introductory and ongoing talks. There are regularly published new series of short talks that can be used as well, now available on CDs as well as tapes. If you need further advice on what tapes or CDs to choose, you can consult your regional or national coordinator or Medio Media.

In fact, any of these talks will nourish and inspire. There are also useful taped talks by other teachers in the same tradition. For more established groups you might adapt some of the longer retreat or seminar sets that have been published, playing a different part of a talk for a number of weeks. The leader of the group should choose the tape beforehand and spend a moment or two introducing its theme to the group before playing it. Of course the group leader or other member could also give a talk from time to time if they feel confident in doing so. And teachings can be read aloud by the group leaders or another group member, either from the texts themselves or from the weekly reading posted on www.wccm.org, which also contains a brief reading underscoring the main teaching to be read following the meditation.

The Meditation. After the teaching there should be a moment of silence while lights are turned down. The meditation period itself can be introduced by a couple of minutes of suitable music, such as Margaret Rizza's or a quiet classical piece. The meditation period is normally 25 or 30 minutes. If the group is new to meditation you could begin with 20 minutes and gradually build up from there. The leader or other member of the group is responsible for timing the meditation, and can signal the beginning and end of meditation with a soft ring of a chime or prayer bowl. There are other ways to signal the end of meditation without making everyone jump out of their skin when the alarm or buzzer goes off at the end. You could use a quiet alarm or a pre-recorded tape of silence with a short piece of music at the beginning and end. Preparing for the meditation period as a time of deep stillness and quiet is an important part of the job of the group's leader but it involves everyone.

After Meditation. There may be a brief reading following the period of silence, preferably repeating a key point in the previous teaching or echoing with a brief passage from another source. The final part of the group is the sharing or discussion session. It doesn't matter if on some weeks people don't feel like talking. Then the group should be concluded quietly and people take their leave. Often though, after a few minutes of sitting in silence, people like to share a reflection or a question. The group leader can often steer the discussion gently by referring to a key point or scripture reference made in the talk or sharing some other related reflection. This should not be a time of debate or controversy, nor should it be a time for analysis of personal problems and other life issues. There are other venues better suited for this.

If there are questions the group leader shouldn't feel obliged to have the answer. Others in the group may have a good response, and, of course, all questions need not be answered immediately after they are asked. Group leaders can get back to members, either privately or at the next session, after further reflection or after consulting Paul Harris' book, *Frequently Asked Questions*. If a question seems unanswerable, it probably is; don't try to answer it. Allow space for the mystery, too. In general, a brief time for sharing reflections helps grow a sense of solidarity and appreciation for the many different gifts and perspectives that help make a group a community.

Know The Essential Teaching

While the regular teaching component of the weekly meeting is critical, in the end the group teaches what can only truly be learned from experience, in silence. But just as it is important to begin each session with a teaching, it is also important for the group leader to feel comfortable in articulating the essential teaching in his or her own words and style. There are of course many ways to convey the same truth, as long as the essential simplicity of meditation is emphasized.

Meditation is as natural to the spirit as breathing is to the body. Deeply rooted in the Christian tradition, it is an ancient spiritual discipline, a simple way into union with the Spirit of Christ. The tradition does not say that meditation is the only or even the best way to pray. It simply conveys the wisdom, at once practical and holy, of daily silent prayer. It transmits the essential teaching of contemplative prayer, first articulated in the early church through the teachings of the Desert Fathers and passed on with special clarity and depth in our time by John Main. This tradition advises the following simple practice:

Choose a quiet place.

Sit down comfortably, with your back straight.

Close your eyes lightly.

Sit as still as possible.

Breathe deeply, staying both relaxed and alert.

Slowly and interiorly, begin to say your mantra.

Continue repeating it gently and faithfully for the whole
time of the meditation.

Return to it as soon as you realize you have stopped
saying it.

Stay with the same word during the meditation and from
day to day.

And remember that the root of all distractions is self-consciousness. In meditation we are, in a real and ongoing way, 'leaving self behind'. The mantra we recommend is maranatha, an ancient Christian prayer from the language Jesus spoke, Aramaic, meaning 'Come Lord'. Repeat the word in four equal syllables, ma-ra-na-tha. Listen to the word as you say it and give it your full attention, but don't think about its meaning. Distractions will come but don't try to repress or fight them. Simply let them pass. When you do find that one has hooked your attention, simply return in faith to saying the mantra. This is the 'work of the word'. Meditate twice a day, ideally in the early morning and early evening. The optimal length of time for meditation is thirty minutes, but might begin with twenty and gradually increase to twenty-five or the full half hour.

Once you have begun this simple daily practice, there are a few guidelines concerning your attitude to the experience that will help you and others go deeper. First, don't assess your progress. The feeling of failure – or success – may be the biggest distraction of all. Do not expect or look for 'experiences' in meditation. You don't have to feel either that anything should be happening. This may seem odd at first, because the experience of silence is so unfamiliar to most of us personally and so alien to our culture. And we are not used to being simple. The silence, stillness, and simplicity, however, do have a purpose. In one of the parables of the Kingdom, Jesus compares the Kingdom to a seed that someone plants in the ground. The person then goes off to live an ordinary life while the seed grows silently in the earth, 'how he does not know'. The same thing happens to us, as the word is rooted evermore deeply in our hearts. And, as in the parable, there will in time be signs of growth. You will not always find them in your meditation itself, but in your life. You will begin to harvest the fruits of the spirit; you will find that you are growing in love. And if you ever stop the practice of meditation, whether for a day or a month or a year, simply return to it again with confidence in the infinite generosity of the Spirit that dwells in and among us all.

Other Forms of Prayer

Meditation – often-called 'pure prayer' – does not replace other forms of prayer. What these are in the lives of different people will depend on their temperament and vocation and the kind of Christian tradition they are formed in. The reading of Scripture, communal prayer and worship and the prayer that expresses itself in physical acts of compassion and works of charity are all irreplaceable elements of a life lived in the way of the gospel. But the forms they take will vary. The practice of meditation is a living foundation for these—not a substitute for them.

Other Faiths

The attitude of Christians to other faiths is, under the guidance of the Holy Spirit, undergoing a historical shift today. Christians no longer arrogantly reject other faiths but are able to revere what is good and holy in them. Dialogue with these faiths impels us to seek new ways of expressing Christian experience alongside traditional theology. The contemplative experience is essential if inter-religious dialogue is to mature. The Christian Meditation group is instinctively ecumenical in this broader sense. Each of its meetings is open to any genuine seeker and it will respond hospitably and gently to others. Although it is not an interfaith group as such it will welcome people of other faiths, or those seeking for faith if they are content to meditate with Christians – whose own faith in Christ as their teacher inspires them to imitate his truth and openness.

If the group concurs it can be a rewarding practice to make contact with other religious groups locally and sometimes to have an interfaith meditation evening together.

Am I The One To Do It?

Starting a new Christian Meditation group is a step of a faith, but it will be an enriching responsibility. Whatever you give you will receive back manifold. Always remember that you are not expected to be an expert or a model meditator. Just a humbly committed one. The teacher is within. His name is 'above all names'. A group becomes a channel of his presence not only to its own members but to all those whose lives they interact with during the week. Like everything else in the life of the gospel, the meditation group does not exist for itself alone. If you can see this you will not be nervous about sharing the gift and you will not be concerned about numbers. You will know that this little community of contemplative faith – in communion with many others around the world – is nurturing the spiritual journey of its members. But also in a world that is becoming too noisy to listen, it is acting as a window of silence to the divine mystery in our midst.

Available Resources

THE WORLD COMMUNITY FOR CHRISTIAN MEDITATION

John Main saw that meditation creates community. Over the past 25 years this insight has taken shape in the growth of a worldwide contemplative network extending to over a hundred countries. There are Christian Meditation Centres in many of these. These Centres serve as focal points for the teaching and life of the community locally and nationally. An annual John Main Seminar is held in which a leading thinker or teacher enriches the Community's contemplative vision of the modern world and its challenges. A Guiding Board in the spirit of the Constitution of The World Community is drawn from different countries and gives direction and assistance to the growth of the Community. A quarterly Newsletter gives spiritual teaching and local and international news of the Community.

SCHOOL FOR TEACHERS

The School for Teachers has been started to help people better understand and accept the gift of meditation in their own lives so as better to share it with others. It would be very enriching to participate in one of the regular Schools that are held in many countries every year. A School weekend experience would help you discern whether to start a group and give you more clarity about how to do it. Later you can participate in a School with members of your group. All that is required to attend a school is personal commitment to the way of Christian meditation, a year or two of sustained personal practice, and a call to share the gift with others.

The School is an experience of encouragement and empowerment. The International Coordinator in London works with National coordinators in other countries. The School consists of three phases: a weekend workshop on the 'Essential Teaching' and offering help with presentation skills; a series of wider-ranging workshops applying the contemplative insight to issues of modern concern; an extended retreat experience in which a guided reflection on one's own spiritual journey may help one to be a better spiritual friend to others. You may contact your national coordinator or the School Coordinator at the International Office in London. The School also has a section on the Community webpage (www.wccm.org).

THE WEBPAGE: *www.wccm.org*

A growing number of people every day are led to meditation by means of the Internet. Many are led to meditation groups near to their homes through this connection as well as finding a further sense of community in the frequently updated news and discussion of The World Community web page. When you start a group let the web page community know. If you have any special events, pass it on. You will also find news of upcoming retreats and workshops in the web page international calendar. There are reports and photos of recent events and often talks or teachings on meditation are posted. There is also a weekly posting of short readings, described below.

MEDIO MEDIA: *www.mediomedia.org*

Medio Media is the publishing arm of The World

Community. A wide range of products, books, audio tapes and videos by John Main and many others may be ordered over the web direct. You can also ask to receive the catalogue by mail and regular email notification of new titles.

Medio Media Publishing
15930 N. Oracle Rd, Suite 196
Tucson AZ 85739 USA
Toll-free: 1-800-324-8305
Fax: 1 520 818 2639

INTERNATIONAL CENTRE OF THE WORLD COMMUNITY

The International Centre of The World Community is based in London. It serves as a central point of communication and communion for meditators and other Christian Meditation Centres worldwide. It coordinates many aspects of the life of the Community such as the quarterly Newsletter, the annual John Main Seminar, visits, retreats and other special events. The team at the Centre is also there to help you personally with any queries you may have and will happily put you in touch with the local community nearest to you.

International Centre
The World Community for Christian Meditation
St Mark's, Myddleton Square
London EC1R 1XX
Tel: + 44 20 7278 2070
Fax: + 44 207713 6346
Email: mail@wccm.org

COCKFOSTERS

The Benedictine Monastery of Christ the King,

Cockfosters, is a community in the city that welcomes meditators from around the world for retreats and visits to share in the prayer life of its monastic and parish communities. The Guestmaster, Monastery of Christ the King, Bramley Road, London N14 4HE, UK (Tel: +44 20 8440 7769)

TAPES FOR MEDITATION GROUPS

A good series to begin with is *Communitas*. There are five sets in this series each set having ten tapes. These are inspiring and moving talks given to meditation groups and ideal for leading your group into a period of meditation. Side A is a talk for beginners and at some point repeats the essential 'how to' of meditation. Side B is for ongoing meditators. A set of six tapes called *In The Beginning* is composed only of talks for beginners. Another set called *Being on The Way* is just talks for more experienced meditators. These and other sets of tapes by John Main and Laurence Freeman can be found in the Medio Media catalogue or ordered directly from the web page (www.mediomedia.org)

BOOKS FOR MEDITATION GROUPS

John Main's *Word into Silence* is an excellent short introduction to the Christian context of meditation. His *Christian Meditation: The Gethsemani Talks* tells concisely how he came to meditation himself. After that *Moment of Christ* and *The Way of Unknowing* would be helpful.

Laurence Freeman's *Christian Meditation: Your Daily Practice* is a good short practical summary and his *Light Within* is also a good introduction. His book *Jesus: The Teacher Within* explores the contemporary meaning of Christian identity in the light of the experience of meditation.

MUSIC FOR MEDITATION GROUPS

An ideal and beautiful music for leading into and out of meditation is that of Margaret Rizza, an English meditator. Her acclaimed CDs include *River of Peace* and *Fountain of Life* and are available from Medio Media (www.mediomedia.org).

WEEKLY READINGS FOR MEDITATION GROUPS

There are readings for meditation posted each week on the www.wccm.org website. The readings usually contain a teaching from John Main or Laurence Freeman, with a brief comple-mentary after-meditation reading from other sources, including scripture, poetry, and sacred texts from other traditions. The readings can be printed out and used in the group itself or given out to members as a support for their daily practice. Each week, hundreds of people around the world receive the readings directly by e-mail; if you would like to receive them, just follow the instructions under the "Weekly Readings" section of the website.

SAMPLE ANNOUNCEMENTS FOR NEW MEDITATION GROUPS

CHRISTIAN MEDITATION GROUP

A Christian Meditation Group meets at (address) each (day / evening of the week) at (time). This form of silent, imageless prayer using a mantra or prayer word is rooted in the Gospel, the letters of St. Paul and originated with the early Desert Fathers of the 4th century. A Benedictine monk, Father John Main (1926-1982) has rediscovered this ancient prayer tradition for contemporary men and women. Today there are over 800 Christian Meditation groups around the world.

Newcomers are welcomed to the group. The one hour meeting includes quiet music, a short taped talk on meditation by Father John Main, 25 minutes of silent meditation, followed by a question and answer period. For further information, (phone number).

CHRISTIAN MEDITATION GROUP

A Christian Meditation Group at (address) welcomes newcomers each (day and time) to a Meditation Group Meeting. This ancient form of Christian prayer, rooted in the Gospel and St Paul, was taught by St John Cassian and the 4th century Desert Fathers, and is found in the fourteenth century spiritual classic, *The Cloud of Unknowing*. Meditation, also known as contemplative prayer, seeks God in the silence and stillness beyond word and thought. A Benedictine monk, John Main (1926-1982) has rediscovered this ancient prayer tradition for contemporary men and women. There are now (number) Christian Meditation Groups meeting weekly in (country). The one hour meeting includes quiet music, a short taped talk on meditation by Father John Main, 25 minutes of silent meditation, followed by a question period.

For further information phone (name, telephone number), or come along any (day and time).

CHRISTIAN MEDITATION GROUP

A new Meditation group has been formed in (city, town or parish) to introduce newcomers to Christian Meditation. Meditation is not something new. Rather it is central to the Christian experience and deeply rooted in Christian tradition. Meditation, also known as contemplative prayer, is the prayer of silence and listening. This is the aim given by the Psalmist "Be still and know that I am God."

To learn more about Christian Meditation, you are invited to participate in a weekly group meeting held at (time) each (day) at (address). For further information phone (name) at (number).

CHRISTIAN MEDITATION GROUP

Newcomers are invited to join a Christian Meditation group which meets each (day), (time), at (address). Meditation is an ancient form of contemplative prayer that seeks God in the silence and stillness beyond word or thought. Benedictine monk, Father John Main (1926-1982) says "In meditation our way forward to this growing awareness of the Spirit praying within us lies simply in our deepening fidelity to the saying of the mantra. It is the faithful repetition of the word that integrates our whole being. It does so because it brings us to the silence, the concentration, the necessary level of consciousness that enables us to open our mind and heart to the work of God in the depth of our being."

For further information, phone (name) at (phone number).

RELATIONSHIP WITH OTHER CONTEMPLATIVE COMMUNITIES

The tradition of Christian contemplative prayer is a rich and broad one with expressions in many different spiritual schools and Christian denominations. To meditate in the tradition that the world Community teaches is to be rooted in a part of this great vineyard. Friendship and cooperation with other communities representing different aspects of this same tradition, such as Contemplative Outreach, is a natural fruit of meditation and also a sign of the peace that it engenders. (See Appendix 4, page 56)

An Outline for
A Six-Week Introductory
Christian Meditation Group

The following outline is meant to help you – as a group leader – to introduce meditation to newcomers to your group over a six-week period. It will help you help others to get going and to persevere long enough to break through into their own understanding. It may be used continuously or periodically during the year or as a refresher for more experienced meditators.

At the Beginning:
Be especially welcoming to newcomers who may be finding the silence of the group a little strange. Whenever possible meet personally with them and explain the basics of how to meditate and tell them they can raise any questions with you personally as well as in the group. It may help to suggest that they 'check in' with you monthly at first. Help them understand that the importance of the weekly meeting is to strengthen their daily practice and help them come to deeper understanding of the way of meditation. Remind them that it will take time for a regular practice to get established in their daily life and not to give up. If they do, they should just start again. Explain the general structure of the group and the centrality of the meditation period together. Help them to sign up for (and contribute to the cost of the International Newsletter. Share a little of your own journey when this seems helpful.

Each week:
Emphasize the simplicity of meditation.
Review the basic 'how to meditate'.
Explain the theme of the week and a short summary of the tape you
     will listen to.

Recommend specific reading.

Have the basic introductory books and tapes available for sale or loan. (All are available from Medio Media at *www.mediomedia.org*.)

Offer handouts such as the basic local, national and World Community fliers.

Have printouts available of the Weekly Readings from the Web page (*www.wccm.org*).

Encourage questions afterwards which you and other members can respond to.

WEEK ONE

The theme is: *What is Meditation?*

Explain how meditation is a universal practice also found in our Christian tradition. It is a discipline not just a technique. There are no difficult theories or techniques to master. Emphasize the stillness of the body and the importance of the twice-daily practice. Prepare them for the encounter with the monkey-mind. Remind them that meditation is the prayer of the heart so all thoughts, including holy ones, are to be left aside. Play one of John Main's talks from his 'In the Beginning' series.

Recommend Laurence Freeman's book, *Christian Meditation: Your Daily Practice.*

Suggested New Testament Reading: *Matthew 6: 5-6*

WEEK TWO

The theme is: *John Main*

Briefly, in your own words, tell the story of his life. He found meditation first in the East then rediscovered the Christian monastic tradition of it and later went on to teach it to lay people. This led to the worldwide community of which the group you are meditating with this evening is a part. Meditation creates community. Tradition is a personal discovery. Each of us has to rediscover it 'in our own experience'. Play one of the *In the Beginning* talks.

Recommend John Main's book, *Christian Meditation: The Gethsemani Talks*.

Suggested New Testament Reading: *Matthew 6: 7-15*

WEEK THREE
The theme is: *The Roots of our Tradition*
Pick up on John Main's rediscovering of the mantra in John Cassian's Tenth Conference and the meaning of poverty of spirit – simply letting go. Explain how Cassian, like the Cloud of Unknowing and the Orthodox tradition of the Jesus Prayer in the Philokalia, emphasize the continuous saying of the word. Distractions are to be let go of, not fought or repressed. This gradually leads into the present moment. All this is a way of discipline but the fruit is liberty of spirit. Use another talk from *In the Beginning*.

Recommend John Main's book, *Word into Silence*.

Suggested New Testament Reading: *Matthew 6: 25-34*

WEEK FOUR
The theme is: *The Wheel of Prayer*
Now that they have been meditating for a while they have been introduced to the prayer of the heart, a new experience for most people. So now ask 'what is prayer?' in the light of this experience. All forms of prayer are valid and meditation does not replace them, although it may simplify them along with everything else in life. In the Christian tradition all prayer leads back to the prayer of the Spirit in the heart. My prayer - by itself - gives way to his prayer. Choose a talk from John Main's set *Being on the Way* or one of the *Communitas* series (side B), but remember to repeat how to meditate, as this introduction may not be on those talks.

Recommend a re-reading of Laurence Freeman's book, *Your Daily Practice*.

Suggested New Testament Reading: *Romans 8: 26-27*

WEEK FIVE

The theme is: *Leaving Self Behind*

What we are really doing as we meditate is a selfless activity. All spiritual traditions describe this as the basic way to find who and why we are. Meditation is a universal and personal quest for truth. Leaving self behind is not a violent or repressive process. It is learning simply to be and to let go of desire and fear. Play a tape from the *In the Beginning* set.

Recommend Laurence Freeman's book, *Selfless Self*.

Suggested New Testament Reading: *Matthew 7:13*

WEEK SIX

The theme is: *Meditation as a way of life*

The early Christians said that the way you pray is the way you live. The fruits of the daily practice appear in life situations and relationships as we live from a deeper inner center. Our religious tradition appears in a new life as well, along with a greater respect for other traditions. Wisdom and compassion are the greatest gifts.

Recommend John Main's book, *Moment of Christ*, or Laurence Freeman's *Aspects of Love*.

Suggested New Testament Reading: *Philippians 2:1-11*

Consider having a special event after this sixth meeting to mark the conclusion of the introductory course and remind everyone that we are all – always – beginners.

APPENDIX 2:

NATIONAL COORDINATORS / CONTACTS
OF THE WORLD COMMUNITY

Australia
Eileen Dunnicliff
Australian Christian Meditation Community
St Faith's Anglican Church
6 Price Avenue
Montmorency
Victoria 3093
Tel: +61 3 5962 1074
Email: edunnicliff@vtown.com.au

Belgium
Agnes D'Hooghe-Dumon
Christelijk Meditatie Centrum
Beiaardlaan 1
1850 Grimbergen
Tel/Fax: +32 2 269 5071
Email:
dhooghedumon@planetinternet.be

Brazil
Ana Fonseca
Crista Meditacao Communidade
Avenida Epitacio Pessoa, 2870 / 502
22471-000 Rio de Janeior – RJ
Tel: +55 21 25235125
Fax: +55 21 24934975
Email: ana.fonseca@umusic.com

Canada
Christian Meditation Community
George Zanette
21 Sara Street
Woodbridge
ON L4L 8P1
Tel: +1 905 856 1765
Fax: +1 905 856 7165
Email: zanette@sympatico.ca

Fiji
Father Denis Mahoney
Christian Meditation Centre
PO Box 3340
Lami
Tel: +679 361106
Fax: +679 361181
Email: frdenis@replac.org.fj

France
Dominique Lablanche
Communauté Mondiale de Méditants
Chrétiens
16 rue des Trois Frères
Paris 75018
Tel: +331 40 31 89 73
Email: dominiquelablanche@wanadoo

Germany
Mariya Plotzk
Weltgemeinschaft für Christliche
Meditation
Untere Leiten 12 d
82065 Baierbrunn
Tel: +49 89 68020914
Fax: +49 89 74424917
Email: hm.plotzki@web.de

Hong Kong
Sean Burke
Maryknoll Fathers and Brothers
44 Stanley Village Road
Stanley
Tel: +852 2813 0357
Fax: +852 2813 7221
Email: spburke@netvigator.com

51

Malaysia
Patricia Por
The World Community for Christian
Meditation
1439 Jalan 17/21-L
46400 Petaling Jaya
Selangor
Tel: +60 3 79587050 (h)
            +60 3 76216695 (w)
Fax: +60 3 79545780
Email: ppor@pc.jaring.my

Netherlands
Ellen Nagtzaam and Marijke Oprinsen
Christelijk Meditate Centrum
Insulindeplein 7
Tel: ++31 013 544 0563

New Zealand
Rev. Richard Clarke
The World Community for Christian
Meditation
PO Box 27
Otaki Railway
Kapiti Coast 5560
Tel: +64 6 364 3551
Email: clarkerr@xtra.co.nz

Norway
Rune Teigland
Verdensfellesskapet for Kristen
Meditasjon
Mannsverk 24
5034 Landas
Tel: +47 55 200900
Email: rute@online.no

Poland
Pawel Pietowski\O Medytacji
Chrzes'cigan'skiej
Ul. Wtodarzewsha
51H m 10
02-384 Warszawa
Tel: +48 602 478 637 (h)
Tel: +48 22 822 5819 (o)
Fax: +48 (22) 828 6350

Portugal
Crista Meditacao Communidade
Tomazia Santa Clara Gomes
R. Luciano Cordeiro, 24, 2.o C
1150-215 Lisboa
Tel: +351 456448
Email: tstaclara@mail.telepac.pt

Singapore
Peter Ng
The World Community for Christian
Meditation
9 Mayfield Avenue
Singapore 438023
Tel: +65 348 6790 (h)
Tel: +65 330 8801 (o)
Fax: +65 348 7302
Email: ngks@gic.com.sg

Sri Lanka
Sister Immaculata Silva
Good Shepherd Convent
Nayakakanda
Wattala
Tel: +94 930 312
Fax: +94 1930255

Switzerland
John Moederle
Communauté Mondiale de Méditants
Chrétiens
2 rue des Barques
Genève 12-7
Tel: +41 22 700 2163
Fax: +41 22 786 3163

United Kingdom
Bill Neeson
The World Community for Christian
Meditation
5 Hillside Way
Weston Favell
Northamptonshire, NN3 3AW
Tel: +44 (0) 1604 411481
M: 07885 083374
Email: bill@ananda96.fsnet.co.uk

Northern Ireland
Sister Evelyn McDevitt
The World Community for Christian Meditation
Ballysillan House
614 Crumlin Road
Belfast, BT14 7GR
Tel: +44 (0) 2890 715 758

United States
Lisa Sita
The World Community for Christian Meditation
192-10B 69th Avenue
Flushing
NY 11365
Tel: +1 718 454 3296
Email: lsita@lagcc.cuny.edu

West Indies
Sister Ruth Montrichard
37 Gittens Avenue
Maraval, Trinidad
Tel: +1 868 622 8830/6483
Fax: +1 868 622 1043
Email: ruth@wow.net

wccm.org
WCCM Web-page Coordinator
Gregory J. Ryan
Email: gjryan@aol.com

CHRISTIAN MEDITATION CENTRES

International Office
The World Community for Christian Meditation
St. Mark's, Myddelton Square
London EC1R 1XX
Tel: +44 (0)20 7278 2070
Fax: +44 (0)20 7713 6346
Email: mail@wccm.org

Centres Throughout The World

Australia
Australian Christian Meditation Community
PO Box 6630
St Kilda Road Central
Victoria 3004
Tel: +61 3 5962 1074
Email: thebrodericks@bigpond.com

Belgium
Christelijk Meditatie Centrum
Beiaardlaan 1
1850 Grimbergen
Tel/Fax: +32 2 269 5071
Email:
dhooghedumon@planetinternet.be

Brazil
Crista Meditacao Communidade
C.P. 33266
CEP 22442-970
Rio de Janeiro
Tel: +55 21 512 3806
Fax: +55 21 294 7995
Email: ana.fonseca@umusic.com

Canada
Christian Meditation Community
Canadian National Resource Centre
7211 Somerled Avenue
Montreal, QC, H4V 1W9
Tel: +1 514 487 5569
Fax: +1 514 489 9890
Email: audreybooth@citenet.

Centre de Meditation Chretienne
Cap Vie
367 Boulevard Ste Rose
Laval, QC, H71 1N3
Tel: +1 514 625 0133
Email: monic@smartnet.ca

Germany
Christian Meditation Community
Untere Leiten 12 d
82065 Baierbrunn
Tel: +49 89 68020914
Fax: +49 89 74424917
Email: hm.plotzki@web.de

India
Christian Meditation Centre
1/1429 Bilathikulam Road
Calicut, 673006, Kerala
Tel: +91 33 495 50395

Ireland
Christian Meditation Centre
4 Eblana Avenue
Dun Laoghaire
Co. Dublin
Tel: +353 1 280 1505
Fax: +353 1 280 8720
Email: tfehily@oceanfree.net

Italy
Centro de Meditazione Christiana
Via Faentina 32
50133 Florence
Tel: +39 055 48 00 29
Fax: +39 055 463 02 76
Email: cristmedit@dinonet.it

New Zealand
Christian Meditation Community
PO Box 27
Otaki Railway
Kapiti Coast 5560
Tel: +44 6 364 3551
Email: clarkerr@xtra.co.nz

Philippines
Christian Meditation Centre
11 Osmena Street
South Admiral Village
Bgy Merville
Pque
MM 1760
Tel: +63 2 824 9595
Fax: +63 2 823 3742
Email: art@pacific.net.ph

Singapore
Christian Meditation Centre
9 Mayfield Avenue
Singapore 438 023
Tel: +65 348 6790
Fax: +65 348 7302
Email: ngks@gic.com.sg

Thailand
Christian Meditation Centre
51/1 Sedsiri Road
Bangkok 10400
Tel: +66 2 271 3295
Fax: +66 2 271 2632
Email: sketudat@mozart.inet.co.th

United Kingdom
Christian Meditation Centre
St. Mark's, Myddelton Square
London, EC1R 1XX
Tel: +44 20 7833 9615
Fax: +44 20 7713 6346
Email: uk@wccm.org

United States
The World Community for Christian
Meditation
United States National Information Center
15930 N Oracle Rd #196
Tucson, AZ 85739
Tel: +1 800 324 8305
Fax: +1 520 818 2539
Email: wccm@mediomedia.org

THE WORLD COMMUNITY AND OTHER COMMUNITIES

The World Community is one among other networks in the world involved in the rediscovery and teaching of the Christian contemplative tradition. Among these there is a close friendship with Contemplative Outreach expressed in this statement by Laurence Freeman and Thomas Keating.

A Joint Statement from
The World Community and Contemplative Outreach

The contemplative communities of Contemplative Outreach and The World Community for Christian Meditation began independently of each other but in interdependence on the gospel tradition about twenty-five years ago.

Both communities grew from the Christian contemplative and apophatic heritage. We therefore share a special respect for the early monastic tradition, represented for example by John Cassian, the hesychasts of the Orthodox tradition and the medieval mystics such as the author of The Cloud of Unknowing. We believe these traditions are living streams and have a significant and urgent value for Christian life today, for the renewal of all the churches and for enhancing the sense of the sacred in the modern world.

It seems to us that the Spirit is awakening the contemplative life among the people of God beyond the usual lay or clerical categories. It also nurtures an experience of communion beyond denominational boundaries. The same Spirit is reminding us of the forgotten treasures of our Christian heritage. Seeing contemplation as a dimension of prayer and of personal lifestyle and finding a contemplative path taught in our own tradition often come as a welcome discovery to many Christians. We believe this discovery and its widening influence needs to be encouraged by all Christian leaders.

Contemplative prayer grows with faith and perseverance and, in order to sustain them, community is born. For both our communities small local groups characterize this growth, both in depth and numbers. We encourage friendship and the sharing of faith between these groups which are committed to be open, hospitable and ecumenical. We believe that greater growth will follow if the groups of each community meet together from time to time to share the silence of Christ and his Word.

The differences of approach to practice, particularly on the issues of the mantra or sacred symbol, are subtle expressions of the richness of the Christian tradition, not divisions. Wisdom and experience however suggest a person persevere in the same practice once undertaken. Living the wisdom of the contemplative path is a matter of faith active in love, not of spiritual techniques. Contemplation is primarily practice not theory and hence requires fidelity to a method or discipline. While recognizing common sources and the ultimate goal for Christian contemplation we also accept that different interpretations and recommendations concerning practice can be equally valid. When differences are respected and similarities shared we are open to true unity and liberty of spirit.

Out of the deepening experience of contemplation the fruits of the Spirit are born in ever-new ways. Charity, compassion and tolerance, peace-making and courage for social justice characterize Christian appreciation and understanding of inter-religious dialogue is also a fruit of the practice of our two communities.

Both our communities are, in the scheme of history, still very young. We are still discovering our full vocation in the Body of Christ. By our spiritual communion and by learning from each other we pray that we will be faithful to the contemplative journey and to the sharing of its spiritual riches with the world.

Laurence Freeman OSB
The World Community for
Christian Meditation

Thomas Keating OCSO
Contemplative Outreach

CONTEMPLATION AND UNITY:
AN ECUMENICAL STATEMENT

We believe that welcome progress has been made recently in overcoming the ancient divisions between Christian churches. The power of the Gospel has often been veiled by the failure of Christians to love one another and to celebrate diversity as a sign of the richness of unity that there is in Christ. We believe, however, that a new era is opening. In these times there is less call for words and ceremonies and more need for the authentic spiritual knowledge that arises through the silence of contemplation.

The spiritual hunger and the widespread suspicion of religion in our society firmly points Christians to this depth dimension of their common faith. The contemplative dimension of the Gospel is not a speciality of particular churches or groups. It belongs to all and summons us all, through the signs of the times, to recover it. Nor is this contemplative dimension of faith to be identified only with the vocation of some to solitude and quiet. It applies equally to the life of good works, prophetic protest against injustice and the patient labour of peace making. Indeed, the integrity and vigour of the Christian life and its witness to the world depend upon the marriage of contemplation and action in the full experience of the mystery of God that passes understanding but it intimately known in daily acts of kindness.

If we cannot understand the silence of Christ we will not be able to understand his words, as an early Christian teacher asserted. Because we are convinced of the urgent need to recover the contemplative dimension in our prayer, worship and ministries, we have committed ourselves to search for ways in which this can be better appreciated by all Christians and by the whole of society. The new Centre for Christian Meditation at St Mark's, Myddelton Square is an ecumenical sign of this resolve to co-operate at that deeper level where unity in Christ is already achieved.

We invite our brothers and sisters in all churches to reflect on and join in this contemplative endeavour and so enrich its vision with their own special insights and traditions.

We believe, too, that in this age of violence and terror, friendship between the world religions is an indispensable foundation of the work for global peace and justice. If this friendship is to be sincere and transformative it also must be rooted in that experience of silence, stillness and simplicity that is the common ground of contemplation.

If we really can achieve a fuller harmony between contemplation and action in this way we will surely better fulfil the greater desire of Christ that we 'may all be one'.

The Rt. Hon & Rt. Revd Richard Chartres,
Bishop of London

Dom Laurence Freeman OSB,
Director, The World Community for Christian Meditation

Cardinal Cormac Murphy O'Connor,
Archbishop of Westminster

Rev. Dr. Leslie Griffiths
Superintendent Minister of Wesley's Chapel